Graham Handley MA PhD

Brodie's Notes on Graham Greene's
Brighton Rock

Pan Books London, Sydney and Auckland

First published 1979 by Pan Books Ltd
Cavaye Place, London SW10 9PG
9 8 7 6 5 4
© Graham Handley 1979
ISBN 0 330 50155 0
Printed and bound in Great Britain by
Richard Clay Ltd, Bungay, Suffolk

Contents

Page reference in these Notes are to the Penguin edition of
Brighton Rock, but as Parts and Chapters are also identified
the Notes may be used with any edition of the book.

To the student

A close reading of the set book is the student's primary task. These Notes will help to increase your understanding and appreciation of the novel, and to stimulate *your own* thinking about it: *they are in no way intended as a substitute* for a thorough knowledge of the book.

The author and his work

Graham Greene, one of the most distinguished and prolific of contemporary writers, was born in 1904. He was educated first at Berkhamsted School, where his father was Head-master, and later at Balliol College, Oxford, where he was awarded an exhibition in Modern History. In 1925 he left Oxford, having published a book of verse while still there. From there he went to Nottingham, where he learned the rudiments of journalism. In 1926 he was converted to Roman Catholicism. For three years he was a sub-editor on *The Times*. and in 1929 his first novel *The Man Within* appeared.

Novels, stories and 'entertainments' (his own term for the writing he regarded as different from his more serious work) appeared at regular intervals. *Stamboul Train* (1932) estab-lished his early reputation; this was confirmed in 1935 by *England Made Me*. There is little point in providing a cata-logue of Greene's publications but it is appropriate to indicate his range and his main concerns. A number of his novels and stories have been filmed, and in 1975 some of these stories were adapted for television in the series *Shades of Greene*. In 1966 he was made a Companion of Honour.

As early as 1935 there emerged one clear indication of his future pattern of work: having travelled in Liberia he pub-lished an account of his experiences in *Journey Without Maps*. From then on Greene's area of interest was global. No con-temporary writer of note has travelled so variously, so widely, nor has any writer succeeded in capturing both local and racial atmosphere more truthfully. One of his most harrow-ing novels, *The Power and the Glory* (1940), is set in Mexico; the action of *The Heart of the Matter* (1948) takes place in West Africa; *The Quiet American* (1955) in Vietnam. *A Burnt-*

Out Case (1961) is back in Africa; *The Third Man* (1950), written as a film-script, is set in post-war Vienna.

Greene's geographical identification is remarkable. Whether the background – and foreground – is Brighton (as in this novel) or a provincial Argentinian town, his touch is sure, his observation discriminating both visually and psychologically. He has the journalist's eye and facility of expression.

It must be said, however, that the great novelist requires more attributes than these; he must be interested in people as individuals, forever fascinated by the multiplicity of human nature in all its degraded and elevated forms, and he has to be concerned for the spirit and soul as well as for the body.

It is impossible to read Greene's novels without becoming aware of his strong Roman Catholic convictions. He has contrasted the Protestant attachment to *good works* with the Roman Catholic emphasis on *faith* and preoccupation with *mortal sin*; and often in his novels examines the problem of sin in the human condition. But behind Greene the Roman Catholic is Greene the humanitarian, aware of frailty and temptation, and of the sordid, deprived lives where religion has neither power, glory nor even effect – apart from the only dimly-comprehended manifestations of ritual. The dogmas of Catholicism are always there, bulking large in the consciousness of Scobie in *The Heart of the Matter*, and in the fears and admissions of the whisky priest in *The Power and the Glory*. In the soured and bitter virginity of Pinkie they are also present. Yet Greene has no propagandist intention, no assertion of right and wrong (though Ida makes her own assertions); he simply presents a faithful record of human nature in action, but never without sympathy.

Although it cannot be said that Pinkie is involved in spiritual decision (though Rose, up to a point, is), Greene identifies sensitively with his creature, and a sympathy is generated that transcends character. It is a sympathy for the state of man: though a character may finish with the technical full-stop, a question-mark is left in the reader's mind beyond the pages of the book. How are they to be judged, those who sinned and killed and followed the dictates of self? Their particular situation may be foreign to us but their reactions occupy that common area of experience, real or vicarious, which colours the world of life and the living world of the imagination.

Graham Greene's mode of expression is journalistic in the best sense, but perhaps we should look more closely at the high degree of technical and imaginative art involved. The reasons for filming so much of his writing are obvious. He has a fine sense of the dramatic, seen in the narrative tension of his novels and stories. There is always something *happening*: violence, the unexpected, the grotesque, the funny; emotions are on or near the surface, yet platitude and cliché are skilfully avoided.

Greene is adept at psychological exposure, and though his characters may be far from home they reflect the early conditioning of that home, and retrospect plays a large part in their lives. Relationships are investigated in scrupulous and telling detail, whether deeply or in passing, and the daily habit which irritates or endears is given a selective focus.

It has been said of Greene that he is too concerned with the sordid and the degrading, rather than with the elevating. There is some truth in this (*Brighton Rock* is a good example). Yet much of life is exactly as he sees it – his approach is neither sensational nor sentimental, but shows a clear awareness of motive and behaviour. Sexuality and spirituality are the pivots of a Greene novel. There may be little beauty in his appraisal but there is truth; and though you may be repelled by an incident or an emphasis you will never be bored.

Brighton Rock does not merely follow the tortured, psychopathic journey of Pinkie from crime to crime; the book traces the beginnings that have foreshadowed the inevitability of a life of violence. There are sudden and effective shifts of focus, but always the immediacy of the situation is conveyed with a taut economy of fact.

When you have read *Brighton Rock*, return to this Study Aid, follow some of the outlines and directions indicated, and see what you can discover for yourself in appreciation of this moving, disturbing novel.

Plot and structure

Plot

The plot of *Brighton Rock* is relatively straightforward, though many pieces do not fall into place until the latter part of the narrative. Fred Hale, in Brighton as Kolley Kibber for the *Daily Messenger*, has to leave cards at particular places and to reveal himself if correctly challenged. But beneath this outward role there is another; he has betrayed Kite (leader of a racecourse mob which lives by taking money from book-makers for protection) to Colleoni, and Kite has been killed by Colleoni's men at St Pancras – though whether they intended to kill him or merely to scare him is not quite clear. What is clear is that Pinkie, seventeen-year-old inheritor of Kite's mantle as leader of this particular mob, is determined to avenge his death; he does so by harassing Fred into a heart attack at Brighton on Whit Monday. Just before his death, however, Fred has 'picked up' Ida; when she learns later that he has died, and sees the newspaper report of the inquest she is suspicious. Thereafter, the plot of the novel hinges on Ida's attempts to unravel the truth and Pinkie's measures to safeguard himself and the mob.

Pinkie faces complications: Spicer has left one of Kolley Kibber's cards at a restaurant. Pinkie goes to this place, meets the waitress who found the card, and realizes she knows that the person who left it was not *the* Kolley Kibber. Pinkie now has two liabilities, the first being Spicer, whom he does not trust and who allows himself to be photographed, and the second the girl Rose, whom he decides (albeit un-willingly) to marry, since despite the fact that they are both under age, a wife cannot be compelled to give evidence against her husband. Pinkie, having outwardly rejected Colleoni's offer to become one of his (Colleoni's) men, betrays Spicer to Colleoni and arranges for him to be 'carved'. But Pinkie is himself carved on the racecourse by Colleoni's men.

He returns to his bed-sitting room to discover that Spicer is not dead, only injured. He pushes Spicer over the banisters (which Pinkie has long complained about), then persuades his solicitor, Prewitt, to testify with Dallow that it was an accident and that he (Pinkie) was not there at the time. He also consults Prewitt about his marriage to Rose.

Ida, meanwhile, has been following clues. Her constant badgering of Rose and her intuition that Pinkie will not stop at one killing means that she comes nearer to the truth and looms larger in their lives as the days pass.

Pinkie realizes he will have to get rid of Rose, and arranges a suicide pact with her, leaving her to kill herself first. She is on the brink of this when she hears his name called, and throws the gun out of the car. Ida has arrived with Dallow and a policeman; Pinkie, feeling he has been betrayed by Dallow, produces the bottle of vitriol, only to have it broken in his own face by the policeman's baton. Blinded, he runs and leaps into the sea. Ida is left to retail her part in the unravelling of the facts; no doubt, future innumerable pub audiences will hear the story.

Rose is left with the possibility that she will bear Pinkie's child; she returns to the room anxious to play the record Pinkie made for her, and which she wrongly believes is a message of love.

Structure

Structurally, the novel is divided into seven parts; the division of these parts is interesting and contributes to the narrative tension of the book. For example, there is an equal division of Part 1. The first section is concerned almost exclusively with the consciousness of Fred, the second with the reactions of 'the Boy' Pinkie, and the visit to Snow's in search of the card Spicer has left. The third section traces the reactions of Ida to the news of Fred's death and her following-up of certain strands that she feels may lead her to the truth – chief among them, it must be admitted, being the relevations of the ouija board!

Part 2 is wholly given over to Pinkie: the first section to his authority (the dealing with Brewer); the second section to his lack of authority (Colleoni's meeting with him and making him feel an inept outsider).

Part 3 follows the progress of Ida in the first section, with the triumph of the horse Black Boy and her visit to the police. Paralleling this, in the second section, the upward movement of Ida emphasizes the downfall of Pinkie – in his attempts to procure the photo of Spicer, and his betrayal of Spicer to Colleoni, which will have disastrous effects for himself.

Part 4 is crucial, with Pinkie carved with a razor in the first section, Ida interrogating Rose in the second and Spicer's 'accident' in the third.

Part 5 is finely balanced between Pinkie's movement towards marriage and Ida's movement towards *him* via The Cosmopolitan and the inadequate Phil Corkery. The link here is Cubitt, who now has information that Ida could use: namely, that Pinkie has killed Spicer. This she learns in the first section of Part 6, while in the second section Pinkie takes, as he believes, a step nearer safety by marrying Rose.

The long Part 7 traces Pinkie's various movements and the gradual awareness of Ida in the first five sections of this Part; the sixth sees Ida and Phil watching Pinkie, Rose, Dallow and Judy; with the remaining sections witnessing the inevitable climax.

By providing two centres of consciousness Greene achieves a split narrative, which, however, is never wholly divided. A comparison might be made here with Dickens's *Bleak House*, where the dual narrators maintain the tension until the final coming together. For when we are with Pinkie we know that Ida is enquiring about him and following her own research. When we are with Ida we are aware that Pinkie is working out the next step to what he fears will be a massacre. Thus the novel never loses dramatic immediacy, and the interactions within the structure compel our attention throughout.

Style and themes

Most novels and stories by Graham Greene are easily recognizable by their style; he is the master of the economically-turned phrase, the crisp and convincing dialogue within the chosen setting. Even in a generally sordid novel he manages to produce a kind of urban poetry – not unlike T. S. Eliot's achievement in parts of *The Waste Land*.

Imagery is used to great effect throughout: war imagery to comment on Pinkie; ship imagery to indicate Ida's preparations for conflict. Animal imagery, too, is associated with the emergence of Rose and her kind from Nelson Place, and for old Crowe when he comes up to work 'the Board' with Ida. In the first three parts of the Textual Notes that follow this commentary, the nature of the imagery and its moral significance is commented upon; thereafter it is up to the student to note the incidence of the images and to assess their significance.

The title of the novel is the first, and central, symbol, for candy 'rock' is lettered all the way through, and this becomes synonymous with the corruption which runs throughout society, and hence within individuals like Pinkie. The word 'rock' is also synonymous with death, since Hale dies in one of those virtually subterranean areas where rock is sold; the rock on which Brighton has, so to speak, been built, has various surfaces and layers capable of penetration and of being undermined. Just how Hale is finally hounded is never described, but the rock with its cheap, 'holiday' style of life is equated with this cheap holiday death.

There is nothing overtly pretentious or deliberately literary about Greene's style. The opening of Part 1 is a case in point: Greene is a splendid conveyor of atmosphere; and Bank Holiday Brighton dominates the first sections. The scene is set, and like a pulse beat within the scene is the erratic rhythm of Hale's consciousness as he moves from fear to temporary security to fear again, as the panorama of the crowds shifts mindlessly about him.

From the general to the specific is the Greene method; he sees and hears with recording eye and ear the interior of a pub, the talk and movement in a tea room, the plush luxury of The Cosmopolitan, or the bed-sitting room. Immediacy is the key, whether it be the crumbs on 'the Boy's' bed, the soap-dish with the pound notes in it, or Ida hugging her bare legs while the yellow-eyed Phil Corkery dozes in his pants beside her.

The public's essential craving for romance and sentiment is reflected not only in the songs but in the cinema, the racecourse, the bar: the sustained atmosphere is one of claustrophobia. The reader recoils from the proximity of such life; this is indeed the major reaction to the theme of the novel. Greene is illustrating how many live; he is not providing any solutions.

Greene's art in *Brighton Rock* lies not merely in the presentation of the outward, but also in a searing exposure of the inward range of moods which constitute our lives. Sometimes the author guides us into the consciousness, as, for example, Hale seeking the security of the pasty girl (Part 1, Chapter 1, p.13): 'Surely, he thought, *this* girl ...' There is the unexpected eruption into the mind without comment, as when the Latin phrases of his religion return to Pinkie, oddly mixed with the facile sentiment of a popular song (pp.50–52). The technique here is sparingly employed; here the book gains by this economy, which makes clear how Pinkie's conscious motives (to take care of everything by killing) are subconsciously undermined by an unacknowledged awareness of what is right. Ida's consciousness is exposed in the same way, but since she is a much more integrated character – she knows what is right and what is wrong and acts accordingly

– the revelations are merely the preparation for action, or a pause while she considers her next move.

Greene, then, is the quintessential dramatic novelist. He creates atmosphere, and balances this with an inward equivalent in which we are shown the consciousness of the characters in reaction to environment and situation. His stories and novels, we have noted, translate to the television or the cinema, and it is easy to understand why this is so. Like Jane Austen's, Greene's dialogue has the ring of truth; we recognize Pinkie, Ida, Dallow and Rose by their words; and if two superior young men enter a car to talk about cars or 'totsies' our ears respond to the meticulous rendering of their words and manner. Consider the following example of Greene observation.

A boy's voice interrupted them. 'So there you are, Fred,' and Hale looked up at the grey inhuman seventeen-year-old eyes. 'Why,' the fat girl squealed, 'he said he hadn't got a friend.' 'You can't believe what Fred says,' the voice said. 'Now we can make a proper party,' the fat girl said. 'This is my friend Delia. I'm Molly.' 'Pleased to meet you,' the boy said. 'Where are we going, Fred?' 'I'm hungry,' the fat girl said. 'I bet you're hungry too, Delia?' and Delia wriggled and squealed. (Part 1, Chapter 1, p.15)

The scene is charged with atmosphere: notice that Fred does not speak; the girls are shallow and silly; the boy controls; and the word 'inhuman' instantly chills.

Greene can be cynical, particularly when he includes quotations or half-quotations either from the Bible or Shakespeare – witness Prewitt's opening of his heart to Pinkie (7,3,208). The overtones are sometimes immediately tragic, as when Hale peers 'out from the valley of the shadow with sourness and envy' (1,1,17).

The use of associative symbol is not confined to the title; notice the horse's name, 'Black Boy' (is not Pinkie – 'the Boy' – himself morally black?) and 'Memento Mori', with its prophetic overtones. Notice, too, the sudden juxtaposition of the unexpected which becomes charged with spiritual significance as, for example, when Pinkie wins a doll and leaves, 'holding the Mother of God by the hair' (p.22). It is this kind of writing that demonstrates Greene's power to suggest the spiritual dimensions beyond the immediate present. Then we note that, when Ida goes to see Molly Pink (p.39), 'A dead fly hung in a broken web.' Pinkie has constructed a web for himself and is gradually caught in it by his own movements. This eye for physical detail is always present: we note the down on Pinkie's cheek, Spicer's corn, the photographs that still live on as a background to the seaside photo that reveals Spicer's substitution for Fred as Kolley Kibber.

A further stylistic device is the use of repetition, not only of phrase but of selected incident: Pinkie reflects again and again on the death of Kite at St Pancras, and each time he thinks of it something more is added to the incident. Pinkie is motivated by the death of Kite just as Ida is motivated by the death of Fred.

Succinct, crisp, slangy, economically metaphorical, giving us the sense and sight, the taste and smell, all these are attributes of Greene's style in *Brighton Rock*. The themes are sufficiently obvious: ugly and squalid conditions breed ugly, perverse and criminal people. In poverty we shall find crime; religion is far away from the social experience and conditions of such people. Pinkie represents wrong but society is largely responsible for making him what he is. Ida represents right, and her sins, whether of the flesh or of obstinacy, are overlooked when the balance is weighed.

Characters

Pinkie

From behind he looked younger than he was in his dark thin ready-made suit a little too big for him at the hips, but when you met him face to face he looked older, the slatey eyes were touched with the annihilating eternity from which he had come and to which he went. (Part 1, Chapter 2, p.21)

Pinkie and Ida dominate *Brighton Rock*, and all other characters are subsidiary to the central battle these two represent; the battle between Good and Evil or, as Ida puts it, Right and Wrong. The fact that Pinkie is referred to as 'the Boy' so often, pinpoints his youth, but it is a youth without innocence. Pinkie means 'the little one', and his lack of stature is often emphasized; for instance, when he runs and leaps into the sea he is compared to a schoolboy. He has a nervous tic; he feels his guts grinding with rage; and he asks repeatedly if he has got to have a massacre. All this adds up to a psychopathic killer – but seen from the inside. So, although we find Pinkie repulsive we are yet able – through our understanding of the childhood that helped create this character – to feel some sympathy for him. We see that he is more intelligent than his associates, but we also see the pathos of the little boy trying to be the big mobster. Because much of his time is spent in retrospect, in which we share, we learn what has turned him against sex: his parents made noisy love on Saturday nights and he, the watcher and listener in the other bed, was already an 'outsider'.

Pinkie is cunning and clever, but also immature; he is bent on killing, yet he has sufficient religious sense to know that he will be damned. He is daring and yet frightened: he can coerce Fred into having a heart attack; break a glass in a pub and say that Fred will pay; push Spicer down the stairs and cover himself by blackmailing Prewitt – yet he is naïve enough to think that his betrayal of Spicer will be enough for Colleoni, and is bewildered, scared, and very small and alone when Colleoni's mob 'carve' him.

Pinkie comes from the lowest level of society, and part of the novel is therefore concerned with demonstrating through him how little chance such a boy will have. He rejects his sordid roots, and he rejects religion – though it is surprising how much he remembers of ritual and words. He regards Kite – killed at St Pancras as a result of Fred's betrayal – as his father; and part of Pinkie's problem is that he has to take over from Kite and *be convincingly seen to take over*. Like Macbeth, he has to go on from deed to deed once he has begun; but this is not all. His sexual attitudes mean that he is vulnerable to the sneer and the inward uncertainty; he hates sex and is fearful of it and ignorant of it too (as he reveals with Sylvie). He can never live up to his own expectations of himself: there isn't time for him to come of age in either the criminal or the sexual sense. He is aware of the contrast between Billy's and The Cosmopolitan, and that difference emphasizes the gulf between himself and Colleoni, between Rose and the girl(s) he would have commanded if he had made the 'big time'.

Divided within, then, because of uncertainty about his sexual performance, divided without by the fact that he is a boy in a man's world, Pinkie lives only to lead and to rule by the razor or the vitriol bottle. His immaturity is shown in several ways: he gives the game away to Cubitt about his own killing of Spicer; drops the flower he is carrying when he is brooding about Rose's supposed betrayal of him; and is naïve in telephoning Colleoni to tell him to deal with Spicer. He slips up on other occasions too, but he imposes a kind of self-confidence on himself which makes him carry through the interview with Colleoni – and one at the police station too – with remarkable aplomb. But the completely irrational (the inheritance of the boy who used the dividers at school – perhaps fear of bullying drove him to it) is never far from the surface. Pinkie longs for the social recognition of the successful mobster, which he will never have: he is refused service at Snow's, and refused a double room at The Cosmopolitan. The lack of love and care, the beginnings of violence and bullying at school, these form the groundwork for Greene's psychological presentation of Pinkie.

Only once does Pinkie show any humour, and yet he has redeeming qualities – a fact that is hard to credit, so horrible and amoral are his reactions. When he visits Rose's parents he is sensitively aware not merely of their moods but of the sordid existence that approximates to his own; he buys Rose, and the motive is self-interest, yet we cannot help being aware of his own past suffering and his truncated life. His appraisal of popular songs (with their sloppy and mindless words), and some of the 'flickers' he sees (with their synthetic love passing for reality), is critical. We feel his deprivation; we realize that he has an enquiring mind, but one that can only be developed in one direction, because of the nature of the world in which he has, not 'grown up', but struggled to survive. That direction is towards escaping his background by proving himself a leader and being unscrupulous when he has to be. He organizes killing and he kills; and he takes a sadistic pleasure in having the vitriol with him and threatening to use it; he seeks refuge in a garage, and hates the middle-class evidences he finds there, feeling an outsider even in this retreat. Yet throughout all Pinkie's fears and plans, deceptions and sexual hostility, runs the thread of his religion – he has committed one terrible sin and can never go back. There is an inevitability about his end, which ensures that some of our sympathy remains with him.

Greene's outstanding achievement with regard to Pinkie is that we are inside his consciousness, twisted, warped, febrile though it is; we experience his inadequacy with Sylvie, his relief when his wedding night with Rose is over; we feel too the constant pulse-beat of a religious influence that might have been, the reiterated words from the dogma, the knowledge that the old woman he sees on the Montpellier Road is one of the saved. Conscience does not prick Pinkie in the sense in which we usually understand the phrase; Greene's presentation is much more subtle than that: Pinkie shows a lust to lead and a lust to kill replacing the more acceptable social lusts of respectability and status that motivate people who have not shared his deprivations. The Boy is thoroughly understood, thoroughly lived with. His consciousness and motivation dominate most of the book, and the careful reader will make a list of the things that Pinkie does and says – and then he will try to find explanations of those things – for they are assuredly there in the text. Pinkie is vicious, sadistic, impulsive, calculating, capable of blackmail, a liar, a psychopath; the sum of these appalling attributes is nevertheless a rounded character of compelling and monstrous fascination, spawned by a society on which he will be revenged – or himself suffer a mindless end. That is Pinkie's fate, but a certain pathos, a consciousness of waste, attend that sordid end.

Rose

one of those girls who creep about, he thought, as if they were afraid of their own footsteps: a pale thin girl younger than himself. (1,2,26)

Rose is the female equivalent of Pinkie in terms of social background and upbringing (or lack of it). She is uncertain and anxious to please, thankful to have a job and to be sleeping-in at Snow's. Mousy, plain, dull, she responds to Pinkie from their first meeting. She has never had a boyfriend, and her little world of romance brings out in her a positive uncompromising loyalty to the young thug who has – quite unintentionally – won her heart.

Rose soon learns what Pinkie is, but she is a Roman Catholic and accepts the fact that she has sinned, that the 'marriage' is a sin, and that what has been done is irrevocable. She resists Ida's attempts to influence her, but occasionally flashes of independence highlight her relations with Pinkie, for she has a terrible insight into herself and her own physical inadequacy. Yet always she reverts to her *need* of someone to love. Like Pinkie, she often recalls the Catholicism of her childhood and – though up to a point she is Pinkie's dupe – the debate continues within her; when Pinkie leaves her with the gun the crucial dilemma of right and wrong takes on for Rose a heightened spiritual intensity.

She has her moments of shame (when Pinkie visits her parents, for example) and of pride (when she feels that she may have Pinkie's baby). Her attempts to fill her new small world are pathetic: her return to Snow's to tell Maisie that she is 'married' is touching; but most heartrending of all is her return, after confession, to the unforeseen horror of Pinkie's message. The reader is spared that final twist of the knife, but for Rose we feel an unqualified sympathy. She is simple, loyal, misguided but caught in the terrible trap of having had nothing and now, held out to her, is something that awakes in her the need to love.

Pinkie enters Rose's life with the false glamour of being, as she puts it, 'famous'. A terrible irony is seen in her hope of a child, who would assuredly grow up with all the disadvantages she has endured. Although it is her religion that lifts Rose above the sordid commonplace she has inherited, the final sentence of the novel implies that it will be impossible for it to sustain her.

Ida

She wasn't old, somewhere in the late thirties or the early forties, and she was only a little drunk in a friendly accommodating way ... She was well-covered, but she wasn't careless; she kept her lines for those who cared for lines. (1,1,6)

Ida – Lily she is first called in her pub role – is the natural opposite of Pinkie. Where he is small and thin she is large and warm, having the capacity for living that he lacks, 'living' especially in the sins of the flesh. To use her own word, she is a 'sticker'. Once she is on the track of something she does not let go until she discovers the truth. Ida has never had children, and consequently she has a protective and motherly attitude towards the men in her life and, initially, towards Rose in her vulnerable and defenceless state. She believes in Right and Wrong – the capitals are hers – and she is incurably sentimental and romantic (again contrasting with Pinkie): singing her ballads from times past; cherishing her sexy letters from Tom; being the life and soul of pub groups. Ida is superstitious, believing in the sort of 'psychic' activity that is afforded by the ouija board. She lives in lodgings in Russell Square, her sparse shelves indicating books read and re-read.

One understands why Greene defined this novel as an 'entertainment' when one looks a little more closely at Ida: she is much more the character in a mystery thriller than one in a psychological drama. To use an old cliché, Ida is the 'tart with a heart of gold'. As she moves into her middle years she becomes an amateur detective and, of course, finds out more than the police do; in this role she can be impetuous, engaging, insistent, and much larger than life. Yet even at this level, Greene gives Ida a kind of psychological consistency. She is intelligent and sensitive; gregarious, perhaps to cover her own loneliness and the frustration of not having had children. She is sensual, finding Phil Corkery's love-making inadequate, and she is dominating, carrying him and others like the policeman in her insistent wake. She has a kind heart, a genuine wish to see that justice prevails. And her behaviour and attitudes have a certain consistency; her concern over Fred in the car is motherly but it is also the concern that she would show to anyone who was down or worried – for Ida's salient feature is that she is the friend of the underdog.

Her intelligence and keen eye for the facts are shown when she sees the newspaper report on the inquest and realizes there is something inconsistent; and we are told that she feels 'a sense of tears' when she thinks of herself leaving Fred to have a wash in the ladies' lavatory. She is independent enough to reject the argument that it is none of her business, and determined enough to seek out the pasty fat girl in the office in Gray's Inn and question her. Her incredible imagination invests the Board with what she wants to see, and the letters are meaningful to her as a comment on Fred, though later she is able to give them a forecasting significance too. Prior to that we have seen her sentimentality at the crematorium, and this sentimentality is extended into practical fact when she decides to back Black Boy. The subsequent winnings make her private investigation possible, and her gradual wearing down of Rose, her intuitive grasp of events (always embellished by a little imagination), her visit to the police station, where she does the real talking, her fine sense of humour, which is not simply coarse, and, above all, her *vital* capacity to live, these are her salient features. She is lovable, endearing, drinks a little too much and extracts a joy from life, having a zest which springs from a generalized love for people. Her role belongs to the thriller, but her large personality irradiates the pages of an otherwise sordid and degrading picture of life.

Other characters

For the most part, the novel is written through the consciousness of either Pinkie or Ida, with one sequence largely devoted to Cubitt and one to Fred Hale. The other characters exist on a functional, rather than a psychological, level; their role is curtailed, either by death (Fred, Spicer), or by their associations with Pinkie or Ida: Cubitt, Dallow, Prewitt and Colleoni on the one hand, Phil Corkery and Old Crowe on the other.

Fred (Charles) Hale is important in terms of the narrative structure and in terms of function, on the lines of 'Crime and betrayal do not pay, for your friends will get you if the police don't'. The small-time Kolley Kibber who has betrayed Kite is a sad, isolated little man; desperate and panic-stricken, he literally dies of fright. His is a useless existence and it is Ida who provides him with the only warmth and (temporary) security he knows. His heartbeat in the taxi frightens her: he, with his mouth on hers, is returning to his mother and to the womb, the security which has always eluded him. Through Fred, Greene is expressing the miserable futility of the non-existence of the small-time gambler and criminal – who will always drift from bar to bar and racecourse to racecourse, never putting down roots, always on the look-out for money, vulnerable to criminal suggestion and thus to injury or death. Fred is, none the less, a sympathetic character.

Spicer is not dissimilar. He pays a terrific price for his one mistake, for he placed the Kolley Kibber card in Snow's; and Rose noted that he bore no resemblance to that national character. Spicer foresees that Colleoni will triumph; broods about escaping from his present situation; allows himself to be photographed – does everything, in fact, calculated to bring down upon himself Pinkie's displeasure and hence betrayal. But Pinkie's 'carving' does not work, for he is himself more injured than Spicer. The latter thinks he will get away to the pub in Nottingham, but Pinkie kills him by pushing him over the banister. Spicer is another sad character, with little or no individuality or ability, cast in the small mould that allows a boy to dominate him.

Dallow is far more positive. Pinkie depends on him but, when he believes that Dallow has betrayed him, turns on him hysterically and viciously. Dallow takes a sadistic delight in dealing with Brewer under Pinkie's razored-nail authority. He has his affair with Judy, gets drunk quickly and is easily led. Although less intelligent than Pinkie, he is aware that Pinkie himself is liable to error. In his drink-befuddled state he is no match for Ida at the end, and goes with her to find Pinkie. Again, there is a certain pathos in his non-life, in the fact that he will never be a leader; that he will be violent and ruthless at the whim of another; and that he lacks moral standards and any depth of feeling. Dallow is an accessory after the fact in Spicer's killing, and backs Pinkie up by swearing that he (Pinkie) was not there at the time. He, too, represents the sordid nature of a life of crime devoid of any redeeming feature.

Cubitt commands rather more sympathy – he at least tries to clear out when he learns what Pinkie has done. Pathetically he goes to Colleoni, is headed off by Crab, is humiliated and turns to Ida; he tells her what he knows, then crawls back to Pinkie. Cubitt is lost: like Fred, he has no roots; like Dallow he needs to drink; but he has no identity beyond that of the easily-used, easily-led small criminal for whom neither side has any respect.

Colleoni is an almost Dickensian caricature. He has made crime pay, he has also given it a certain respectability. He has not soiled his hands with Kite – others' hands have been soiled for him. He has not been on a racecourse for years, but razors are used there on his behalf. He has the trappings of culture: his suite at The Cosmopolitan is a reflection of the life-style he has achieved; champagne, flowers, grapes, a gold cigarette lighter are the measures of his status. Pinkie envies him but could never emulate him. Colleoni is not in the picture long enough to be psychologically integrated; he belongs to an 'entertainment', but he symbolizes the frightening amorality of power achieved by money alone; how Wrong can live side by side with Right; and how an evil world can be painted over with a gloss of respectable leisured existence.

Prewitt the lawyer, on the other hand, exists in a real world as an individual who has endured the insults of magistrates and prosecutors for many years because of his attachment to the criminals he defends. With Pinkie he finds himself in deeper water than even he could have imagined: he is in the dubious position of supporting Pinkie's story about Spicer under threat of being himself blackmailed. He does so, but is broken by the implications, and when Pinkie visits him to suggest a holiday he agrees, for a suitable payment, to go. But before that he reveals to Pinkie the bitterness of his life and his 25-year-old marriage, interspersing his narrative with quotations.

Prewitt, too, is isolated, his talk covering a sensitive nature and a need for the love he has never had. His background contrasts sharply with Pinkie's own and he cannot forget that it is incumbent upon him to be respectable – which he is not. Once again, as with so many of Greene's characters, we feel a certain pity. Prewitt arranges Pinkie's marriage, with suitable clichés and badinage; but he can never rearrange his own, and this is his tragedy.

Phil Corkery is never more than caricature, as his name suggests. Although he has long had his eye on Ida, her full-blooded sexuality is too much for him. And he finds her quest for Fred's killer equally exhausting; Ida doubts whether he will pay her much attention again.

Chapter summaries and textual notes

Part 1

Chapter 1

Hale, as Kolley Kibber, is in Brighton for the Whitsun Bank Holiday; his task is to leave cards at specified places as part of the ritual of the *Daily Messenger* identity game.

Hale has a presentiment that he is going to be killed, so whenever possible he keeps with the crowds. He goes to a bar and is accosted by a boy, later identified as Pinkie. He also notices a happy woman, a good-time type, who is very slightly drunk. Hale tries to buy off the boy but the latter leaves after deliberately breaking a glass, for which he says Hale will pay. Hale watches the woman, Lily, talks to her briefly and then leaves. He makes for the sea front, then takes another road. He sees a red-haired man called Cubitt, and goes on to the West Pier. Realizing that it would be a safeguard to have a witness with him, he tries to pick up a girl – any girl – but without success, for he has no companion for her friend.

This is soon remedied when Pinkie appears, calling Hale 'Fred' with great familiarity. Hale, terrified, leaves hurriedly, but is in turn picked up by the accommodating Lily, who tells him cheerfully that she has lost her bag containing all her money. Hale remains with for her company and sympathetic conversation, as well as for protection, and advises her to back a horse called Black Boy, which is running at Brighton the following Saturday. She reveals that her real name is Ida. They take a taxi, and Hale discovers they are being followed. Hale feels ill and nearly collapses. They get out at the entrance to the Palace Pier. Ida goes to the ladies' lavatory for a wash, despite Hale begging her not to leave him; but when she reappears he has disappeared.

Victoria London rail terminus, with regular fast train service to the South Coast.

Queen's Road The interested student will 'plot' his own Brighton plan by working out the various locations; if you can get a map of Brighton, so much the better, but Graham Greene's superb sense of locale and atmosphere is evident throughout this novel, (as, indeed, in his other books). It is one of the major facets of his approach.

miniature motors i.e. replicas of cars.

an aeroplane advertising something for the health A common sight in the 1930s was an aircraft leaving a written smoke trail advertising some commercial product, possibly a proprietary medicine. In view of Hale's health, and Pinkie's, this is an ironic glance at the main action of the novel.

sentry go i.e. tour of duty.

Kolley Kibber A ridiculous parody of the name of the famous actor-manager and dramatist who was part-proprietor of Drury Lane theatre. He lived from 1671 to 1757.

There were reasons why We later learn that he has probably been responsible for the death of Kite.

like a twisted piece of wire Greene is master of the commonplace image, particularly with the hint of a sordid association.

the ghost train In the fairground, this is a ride with supposedly frightening sights, like the skeletons mentioned here.

the sticks of Brighton rock Note how cleverly this is repeated at critical moments in the narrative.

felt his kinship i.e. his sense of companionship (with the crowd).

peep-shows Small exhibitions of pictures viewed through a lens, but perhaps here meaning any suggestive entertainment.

her lines i.e. the outlines of her figure.

lead trough i.e. in the bar, behind the counter.

The Australian gold rush We suspect that this is a deliberate exaggeration. The actual date was back in the 1850s and 1860s.

old and mild A type of beer.

blown charm i.e. faded.

loosened like handcuffs The image here is Hale's, but it is a recurrent one in the text, and carries its own moral weight.

down Fine short hair, first growth of hair on the face.

like an old man's A number of images characterize Pinkie, but always there is stress on his age – either by direct reference or, as here, by contrast.

We met ... I thought he would shun me Note that here, as elsewhere in the novel, the songs are a commentary on the main action. Consider this quotation in relation to Hale and Ida.

buer's i.e. a common woman, one who keeps doubtful company.

fiver Five pound note.

rivall'd its whiteness i.e. I was pure, a virgin (a quote from the song sung by Ida).

the long pilgrimage behind him i.e. his life.

damned i.e. he would not. There is, later, considerable play on the religious connotations of the word.

mob Gang (of criminals).

scamped i.e. didn't do it (the job) thoroughly.

the Old Ship Celebrated Brighton pub.

Back to the womb The whole sequence shows Hale desperately seeking security.

queer i.e. pale, sickly, as if about to faint.

a thick forest ... his poisoned ambush Fine image, since it suggests the 'jungle' of the Brighton underworld.

pastiche Something made in the style of an original.

Del Ray perm i.e. a particular kind of permanent wave for the hair.

lost ... one side of the body ... its head aside delicately like a dowager Fine contrast – the animal in the prime of life, the man broken and degraded by injury or ill health.

Razor blades Even this is ominous, since 'carving' is the basic aggression of the mob – and this is how Kite was disposed of.

en brosse i.e. standing up on end, like a brush.

not front-page stuff i.e. not important enough to make the headlines.

tablets A reference to the fading smoke-writing of an aircraft.

the corridor carriage i.e. carriage on a train with corridor.

perms i.e. permanent waves, a method of curling hair, used less frequently today than formerly.

thenk you Thank you. Note the affectation.

from town i.e. London.

fresh Impertinent, cheeky.

sundaes Ice cream topped with fruit, nuts etc.

splits i.e. banana, cream and ice-cream concoctions.

got twopence i.e. to pay for the hire of the deck-chair.

pinched i.e. took, stole.

ten bob Ten shillings (50 pence).

pulled my leg Played a joke (on me).

a sticker where right's concerned i.e. I don't give up until I've got justice – no idle boast on Ida's part, as she is to prove later.

Ida ... Grecian name Ida was the name of two mountains, and 'woody Ida' near Troy was the scene of the rape of Ganymede and also the place where the nature goddess Cybele was worshipped.

the valley of the shadow Note the deliberate biblical echo – 'the valley of the shadow of death' (Psalm 23).

From hand to mouth i.e. from day to day, as best I can.

it was in the dark he had met Kite There is a moral tone here, for the mob operate in moral darkness.

flutter Gamble.

stuffed up i.e. pasty-faced, lacking air.

ring ... shot She is speaking of side-shows e.g. hoop-la and shooting galleries, and small-time entertainment, as distinct from big spending.

1925 Morris The car, with Cubitt, we later learn, following them.

throw up the sponge i.e. give in, surrender.

kidding Joking.

That's a boy i.e. a good boy.

a watch In view of the importance of time to Pinkie and the mob, this is another casual underlining of the emphasis.

geezer Slang for 'fellow', 'person'.

Lord Rothschild said to me This is the refrain which Ida constantly recurs to. Rothschild represents the legendary banker and financier and hence 'riches' – the lure for the poor girl in the 'alley'.

Chapter 2

The Boy goes on to the Pier, checks the time as a quarter to two, and tries a few shots in a shooting gallery. He wins a doll, goes to the sea terrace and waits for his friends, giving the waitress the prize he has won. They arrive, the Boy orders fish and chips and tea; then they review what has been done. Obviously Hale is dead, but his cards have been put in various places, to indicate that he was (supposedly) alive until 2 o'clock.

While they are talking the clock strikes two; Spicer has placed one card at Snow's and Pinkie is worried by this. He decides to go and retrieve the card. He meets the waitress who has found it, and who reveals that she didn't challenge the man who left it because he did not look like Kolley Kibber. This of course is just what the boy had feared, particularly as the girl says she would recognize the man who left the card if she were to see him again. The boy makes up his mind to keep friendly with this waitress.

annihilating eternity i.e. the degrading and sordid existence from which he came – an 'eternity' to anyone who lives through it. Again there is a religious overtone.

quoits A game played with rings, which are thrown over uprights, thus scoring points.

like Virgins in a church repository The image is casual, but prepares us for Pinkie's catholicism – and, if you like, the stress on his own virginity.

'Have you got the time This the first occasion when Pinkie makes a point of *using* the stallholder – the second is later when he drives off with Rose in the Morris, ostensibly to their joint suicide.

phoney alibis Unconscious irony, since an alibi is exactly what Pinkie is set on establishing. 'Phoney' is 'false'.

as a rock Note the repetition of the word 'rock', an underlining of the title.

holding the Mother of God by the hair A powerful image, which suggests that Pinkie's way of life is itself a desecration, an unchristian and degrading thing. But note the superb economy of the phrase, which condenses a wealth of association.

His fingers pulled absent-mindedly Pinkie's reflexes are an index to his psychopathic tendencies, and the reader will notice how often Graham Greene refers to this.

reel Real, proper.

tick Pulse-beat, nervous twitch.

grinding at his guts like the tide Note how often Pinkie is compared to part of the environment, almost as if man and nature are to be permanently identified with each other.

children before his ageless eyes Another reference to Pinkie's old age-in-youth – and the eternal nature of his criminality.

planted him i.e. in a particular place.

fussed Worried, concerned.

polony A slang term for 'girl', with degrading associations.

a half i.e. ten shillings (50 pence).

tarts Usually, prostitutes; here simply 'girls'.

Afternoon moved across the water An unexpected arresting sentence, typifying Greene's sudden switch to a wider perspective.

young ancient poker-face 'Ageless' again, and without expression.

vox humana Organ stop with tones supposed to resemble the human voice.

he smashed a salt-sprinkler Again an underlining of his capacity for violence – witness the broken glass used as a threat with Hale.

cold-eyed, acquisitive, ash-blonde Note the unusual combination, another stylistic trick of Greene's.

dapper Neat, smart.

They freeze you i.e. they act frigidly, coldly.

Chapter 3

Ida is having a drink in Henekeys. She learns of the death of Kolley Kibber, and realizes from a photograph in the paper that Fred was Kolley Kibber. But she has some suspicions of the report of the inquest on Fred, and wonders why he was found dead where he was. She sets off on her own private quest, and goes to the crematorium to see the last of Fred disappear. She sets off for London, and arrives at an office in the Gray's Inn Road, the work-place of the fat girl Fred nearly picked up. This girl has given evidence at the inquest. Ida tries to learn something of Pinkie from her, then returns to her 'digs' in Russell Square. Ida consults her Board – she has a strong tendency towards spiritualism – and interprets the message she receives in the way that she wants. She is now convinced that Fred, or Charles, was driven to his death, despite the 'natural causes' verdict at the inquest.

broke i.e. cut across.

Belisha beacons Flashing orange lights fixed to mark pedestrian crossings, and named after the Minister of Transport who introduced them in 1934, Sir Leslie (later Lord) Hore-Belisha (1893–1957).

White Horse A brand of whisky.

Ruby A type of port wine.

a bit on the horses i.e. a bet.

a mug's game i.e. fit only for a fool.

he wasn't trying it on i.e. he wasn't pretending.

she was back at Brighton i.e. in her memory.

David Copperfield The novel by Charles Dickens, originally published 1848–50, successfully filmed in the 1930s with W. C. Fields as Mr Micawber (and has, of course, been filmed for both cinema and television since the thirties).

talk of suicide ... life assurance Life insurance policies normally include a clause which says that payment will be withheld in the event of death being due to suicide.

plus fours Long wide knickerbockers, so named because to produce the overhang the length has to be increased by four inches.

beats me i.e. I don't understand why.

hieroglyphics Figures of objects standing for words, symbols used by the ancient Egyptians.

flickers i.e. pictures, cinema.

her friendly and popular heart Once again the linking of associations – Ida's warmth and the fact that she gets on well with everybody.

something fishy Suspicious.

Midland Regional A station of the BBC before and during World War II.

there i.e. at the funeral.

plaques ... like school war memorials i.e. in memory of the dead.

National Programme The main BBC broadcasting channel in the 1930s.

New Art doors If literally translated into the French name for 'New Art', these doors could be in the 19th-century 'Art Nouveau' style, which was again fashionable in the 1920s (not 30s) and is once again much admired today. However, the chapel of a newly built crematorium in this 'bright new suburb' of the 1930s would be more likely to have doors in the style called 'Art Deco', very popular in the 1930s and which has also enjoyed a (mercifully!) fleeting vogue in recent times.

like little pats of butter Note the irony of this domestic image, in view of the fact that Fred had no domestic life.

Truth is beauty An unconscious and inevitably clichéd echo of Keats's 'Beauty is Truth, Truth Beauty, that is all/Ye know on earth, and all ye need to know'.

like a conjurer ... nine hundred and fortieth rabbit Heavy irony, but with just an element of truth.

Californian Poppy Widely advertised (and cloying) perfume of the thirties and forties.

ouija boards These are lettered with the alphabet and other signs, and are used with a movable pointer to obtain messages in spiritualistic séances. As we shall see, Ida has her own ritual.

ectoplasm The supposed viscous substance emerging from the body of a medium during a trance.

séance Meeting of those investigating or demonstrating spiritualistic phenomena.

upper life i.e. the life beyond.

Life was sunlight This whole sequence underlines Ida's warm and comfortable nature, her living for the good things in life, not materialistically but humanly.

sky sign ... Do you use Forhans Sign writing in smoke from aircraft again referred to. Forhans was a popular brand of toothpaste.

an eye for an eye ... Vengeance was Ida's Two biblical references are involved here: the first, Matthew, 5,38; the second, Romans, 12,19.

sparked i.e. from the overhead tram-cables.

Charing Cross Station Main line London terminus.

Strand Important and fashionable London thoroughfare.

Stanley Gibbons's World-famous stamp dealers, who issue an annual catalogue for collectors.

dray A horse-drawn cart, used by brewers for transporting barrels of beer.

Trafalgar Square At the top of Whitehall, between the Strand and Leicester Square, and having as its centrepiece the fountains and the statue of Nelson. The student should consult a map of London to trace Ida's route through St Martin's Lane, Seven Dials and Gray's Inn, and then to Russell Square.

natty suitings i.e. smart suits.

like a row of lights Note the sudden, arresting nature of the image.

Tur'ble i.e. terrible.

raffish Disreputable, dissipated.

a card i.e. a wit; a 'personality'; a knowing, artful, usually successful person.

special terms Concessions.

Epsom Obviously the reference is to the races.

a bottle of fizz Slang for 'champagne', or sparkling wine.

lay a couple i.e. bet two pounds.

Two quid Two pounds.

like a cigarette smoker's fingers Again note Greene's casual
yet sharp use of the commonplace image to underline the sordid
and the ordinary.

jaunty and ancient despair Again the paradox of linking two
apparent contradictions; finely and economically done.

A dead fly hung in a broken web Another symbol of decay
and death. Pinkie is later to dismember a crane-fly (which
Greene calls a 'leather-jacket' – see our note p.46).

Woman and Beauty Women's magazine of the period.

blarney i.e. bluster, spin a story.

digs i.e. lodgings.

dunning him i.e. pressing him hard for money he owes.

freehanded Generous.

The dewlaps of the commercials drooped i.e. the
commercial travellers lowered their chins (probably in despair at
not having sold much).

Eastbourne, Hastings South coast seaside resorts.

Aberystwyth Seaside resort and university town in mid Wales.

Edgar Wallace Best-selling thriller writer of the time
(1874–1932).

Netta Syrett A romantic novelist.

The Good Companions The best-selling novel that established
the reputation of the distinguished author and dramatist,
J. B. Priestley (b.1894). Written in 1929, it describes the ups
and downs of just the kind of concert party one would expect to
find on Brighton Pier.

Sorrell and Son A novel by Warwick Deeping (1877–1950).

short-sighted pit-pony eyes Again a casual image, but
effective since old Crowe appears to come from underground
into the light.

plumes Ornamental tufts of black feathers which decorated the
horses' foreheads at horse-drawn funerals.

like a beetle Again the image is a sordid one.

Part 2

Chapter 1

The Boy warns Spicer to keep away from Snow's, but Spicer is obviously nervous over the killing. Pinkie carries vitriol in a bottle in his pocket, intending to use it against Rose (the waitress who found the card) if he has to. When Rose appears, the Boy tries to dissuade her from showing any interest in the Hale affair, and of course he also tries to convince her that Spicer was Kolley Kibber. He mentions the vitriol to her; then they go to Sherry's, watch the dancers and listen to the music. Pinkie reveals his sadistic tendencies when he calls the girl 'green' for her romantic attitude towards love, but they learn that they have a certain amount in common – for one thing, they are both Roman Catholics. Later, the Boy goes back to his bed-sitter and finds the gang there; he determines to deal with a man called Brewer who has not paid his 'subscription' (protection money); he also tells them that he will 'take care' of the girl; Dallow and Pinkie go to see Brewer, who has a sick wife. Pinkie slashes Brewer with his razored thumbnail, and Dallow collects the money. It is obvious that the biggest mobster and racketeer of all – Colleoni – will now be involved when Brewer tells him what has happened. In addition, Rose telephones to say that a woman (we suspect it is Ida) has been making enquiries about Hale's death.

the cat gut vibrating in the heart Note the effect music has on Pinkie; it may be that there are religious associations here too (church music – hymns, for instance).

milky Afraid, cowardly.

A break i.e. a piece of good fortune.

forking his mouth Again note the directness of the association: lightning in the background; and forked lightning is the most dangerous – just as the Boy is at his most dangerous now with the vitriol in his pocket.

blower i.e. the telephone.

Three sixes i.e. the phone number.

nosy Inquisitive.

if you get around i.e. if you move about successfully in various circles.

rumba South American dance.

like a mole into the daylight Compare this with old Crowe's emergence when he visits Ida's room to help her consult the Board.

Everest tricycle The large refrigerated ice-cream tricycle was a familiar sight in the 1930s.

goggled Rolling (her) eyes about.

the two-backed beasts i.e. the dancers. But the description smacks of Pinkie's sexual fears and prejudices.

crooner Singer.

like a dictator ... like the official news Note the comparisons – both commenting on the nature of the society in which they live.

Music talks Note the triteness of the words, the typical twisting of the popular song that 'cons' listeners into a particular mood.

stirred in his brain like poetry A fine ironic comparison – in deprived lives the only poetry is a cheap refrain like this one.

watchdog An ominous word, anticipating the role of Ida in the story.

Armistice Day November 11th, celebrated annually in memory of those killed in the two World Wars.

the troops turned to stone i.e. still, immobile – but note the effectiveness and economy of the image.

Grace Fields funning,/The gangsters gunning Gracie Fields is the legendary Lancashire girl who rose from a factory background to be a singing star, but 'gangsters gunning' looks at the films of the period and, ironically, at a little gangster like Pinkie.

green i.e. inexperienced.

soft i.e. weak.

like a live coal in his belly Again an ironic image.

nails ... splinters ... razor blade The symbols – and tools of violence – for Pinkie from boyhood to manhood.

Agnus dei ... dona nobis pacem Lamb of God, who bears the sin of the world, give us peace.

credo in unum Dominum I believe in one God.

The banister shook under his hand An unobtrusive way of indicating the importance of this in the Boy's mind – it is later to provide him with an excuse.

carve 'em up i.e. use razors on them.

lay off i.e. do nothing.

a squirt A paltry, contemptible person.

jerry Chamber-pot.

the sub i.e. the payment (which Brewer owes).

contorted with ague i.e. twisted with shivering.

close her clapper Shut her mouth.

A welsher i.e. a bookmaker of disrepute who dodges paying out the 'winnings'.

Kite was croaked i.e. killed.

I've got protection i.e. I've got people who will protect me (against you).

Boy and cat, they didn't stir Note the connection of man and animal – both, the implication is, in a sordid jungle.

the tide had turned An ominous phrase suggesting that it has turned against Pinkie and the small mob.

indiscriminating fidelity i.e. mindless loyalty.

mug Fool (but here affectionately said).

bogies i.e. policemen.

all in i.e. exhausted.

and get Clear out.

like the monoliths of Stonehenge Note the ironic comparison between the racecourse – temporary sport and pleasure and crime – and the permanent record of history.

Chapter 2

Pinkie gets a letter from Colleoni asking him to call and see him at The Cosmopolitan (Pinkie himself is P. Brown,

Secretary of the Bookmakers' Protection Association). Colleoni is surprised when he sees how young Pinkie is; he offers him a job, which the boy declines. Colleoni is a man of wealth and elegance, well removed from the sordid life Pinkie leads; and obviously he has had something to do with the murder of Kite. When Pinkie leaves, a plain-clothes policeman approaches him, but at the station he learns that Brewer has withdrawn the charge against him. The Inspector warns him to keep the peace at the racecourse, but Pinkie feels himself insulted – and he also feels, inside himself, a need for more killing.

the falling of a shutter Part of Greene's technique is its cinematic quality – events and reactions are 'photographed' – and here the image of the camera is used to define the Boy's sleep.

a cachou A scented sweet used to disguise breath odour.

keep off that bitch i.e. leave her (Billy's wife) alone.

small tinted creatures i.e. their girls – with made-up faces and, possibly, dyed hair.

racing models Fast cars.

an acre of deep carpet Note how the size is stressed, to contrast with Pinkie's bed-sitter.

Louis Seize In the style dating from the time of the French King Louis XVI (1754–93), who was guillotined by the French revolutionary mob.

Walking on glacé tiptoe Colleoni was tiptoeing in his *glacé* (highly polished – perhaps patent-leather) shoes.

untimely tiara Unsuitable ornamental coronet.

chinoiserie i.e. Chinese art.

They rose angelically towards peace Heavy irony in this innocent image – Colleoni and Pinkie are both corrupt.

Pompadour Boudoir Named after Madame de Pompadour, famous French court beauty and mistress of Louis XV (1721–64).

'Gue The end of the word 'Montagu'.

Napoleonic crowns i.e. stamped on the couches.

push i.e. aggression.

controlled by Greenwich i.e. maintaining Greenwich time.

buttons on a desk Indicating power – having the means whereby to summon other people to you.

the grubby hand against the skyline signalling to the bookie Tick-tack or manual semaphore-type signalling of racecourse touts.

half-crown enclosure i.e. popular, cheap part for public, costing two shillings and sixpence (12½p).

Napoleon the Third ... Eugénie Emperor of the French, and his wife, the Spanish Princess. Napoleon III lived from 1808 to 1873.

a little doggish i.e. naughty, suggestive.

seraglio Walled palace containing a harem, or merely a reference to the harem of a sultan.

'this is Right and this is Wrong' These standards motivate Ida to discover the truth.

bury him in lime The traditional way of burying a criminal executed within the prison walls.

the Big Four i.e. the four senior Scotland Yard officers responsible for dealing with major crimes.

a picture postcard stuck up on the pier Not only another reference to the camera technique, but also a look forward to the picture taken of Spicer which is so vital to the unwinding of the plot.

They caught a murderer once And they are to do so again, is the irony of this statement.

wide i.e. bright, intelligent, clever.

the tote The totalizator, a betting machine.

Aertex drawers Brand-named underpants of an open-weave cotton material.

a racket i.e. a criminal activity.

He trailed the clouds of his own glory after him: hell lay about him in his infancy A deliberate, ironic twisting of Wordsworth's famous lines in the *Ode on the Intimations of Immortality* ('Heaven lies about us in our infancy ... Trailing clouds of glory do we come/From God, who is our home').

Part 3

Chapter 1

We go back to Ida Arnold, who places a bet with Tate on Fred's tip, Black Boy. Tate receives a phone call from Colleoni; Ida learns later that Colleoni is the mobster who ousted Kite, and that Kite's mob is led by a kid of seventeen (obviously Pinkie). Ida follows her intuition and confronts Rose, probing to find out more about Kolley Kibber. Rose almost gives the game away by saying that the man who left the card wasn't so small, which Fred assuredly was. Ida tells Phil Corkery what she has discovered, and despite his advice that she should stay out of it, she goes to the police. The inspector, apparently sceptical, allows her to see the medical report on Fred; the police regard the case as closed, but Ida returns to the Palace Pier with the idea of starting from the place where she last saw Fred.

ewer Pitcher, water-jug with a wide mouth.

sinews of war Flexing of muscles ready for the battle.

Gold Flake Brand of cigarette.

through the wrong end of a telescope i.e. he is the reverse of what he appears.

red money-spider's web across the eyeballs Fine observation, appropriate in view of his trade, and showing the veins too.

a packet A lot of money.

nicker Pounds.

like a large toad Another vivid image, suggestive of slime and hence the underworld.

the Channel The English Channel.

Douro port i.e. from that area in Portugal.

like a shrimp in the sunlight Another fine image.

larrup Beat.

to pick i.e. choose from the menu.

ready to drop i.e. tired out.

Brighton Belle A celebrated pleasure steamer on daily cruises.

No closing hours at sea i.e. there are no licensing hours.

blew into i.e. entered.

don't open till six Evening licensing hours in the 1930s would not begin until 6 p.m.

Camaraderie Good fellowship.

like shutters before a plate-glass window This time almost a death image, a shutting out of light, a variation of the 'camera' image used to describe Pinkie's sleep.

an eye for an eye This phrase almost becomes Ida's theme.

supernumerary Beyond the usual number.

lit i.e. drunk.

tube lift i.e. the lift at an underground station.

carnality Sensuality, sexuality.

planchette Similar to the Board used by Ida.

Straight from the horse's mouth i.e. a reliable tip.

huckster Trader.

the heavy traffic of her battlefield The image is continued, and is expressive of Ida's aggressive and determined spirit. Ironically, Spicer is within reach at this moment of her 'guns'.

Chapter 2

Spicer meets Crab, who is now employed by Calleoni; Crab scares him by saying that Pinkie is now at the police station. And when Spicer returns to Billy's he takes a call from Rose, who has telephoned to tell Pinkie that Ida has been asking for him. Spicer himself goes to the pier, deeply worried by the situation.

Afraid we'd lamp you ... your mug? Scared we'd spot you if you didn't have your face changed?

as how he was left-handed One of the few examples of natural humour in this novel.

a close-up of a screen Again note the cinematic effect.

nark Informer to the police.

grassed i.e. betrayed, gave information.

his pile i.e. his fortune.

gaff i.e. affair, enterprise.

vulcanite spitting noise i.e. the ringing of the phone.

simulated fury Pretended rage.

a thin doll's voice By association, this looks back to Pinkie
  winning the doll – and he has won this 'doll' too.

If he did squeal . . . their own coin If he did betray them, he
  would only be doing what they would have done.

yellow Cowardly.

a cheap photographer with a box camera One of the
  significant moments in the novel, for much hinges on it.

like a scared bird caught in a cathedral A finely observant
  image, which also reflects on the lack of spirituality of the life
  being described.

took the drop i.e. was hanged.

Chapter 3

Pinkie goes to Snow's, but doesn't succeed in getting a table;
Rose tells him she has phoned him, and has spoken to
the man who left the card. They go out into the country
for a ride, and Rose tells him about Ida. Rose is obviously
infatuated with Pinkie. They kiss, clumsily on his part, then
go back to the pier, where a photographer tries to take their
picture. The Boy sees Spicer's photograph displayed, and
Rose recognizes him. Pinkie tries to obtain the photo, but
doesn't succeed. He goes back to see Spicer, and tells him
that he will have to disappear; but first he must help Pinkie
at the races. Pinkie then betrays Spicer on the telephone to
Colleoni, little suspecting that he himself may reap a different
reward from the one he anticipates.

soured virginity A too-long-standing virginity, without purity
  and soured by neglect.

pale-green sea . . . shabby side of England Note the
  personification, making the land more real than the people.

the draught might never be offered i.e. of poison, the Boy's own image for commitment and sexuality.

walking out Going steady, courting.

his virginity straightening in him like sex An ironic description, for Pinkie is afraid of sex, yet the image here implies the erection of the male sexual organ.

Salvation Army gaff Here 'gaff' probably means a hut or building, used by the Salvation Army as a local meeting place.

a Roman i.e. a Roman Catholic.

all dandy i.e. going well, all right.

take any stock i.e. value, set any store by.

Between the stirrup and the ground 'Betwixt the stirrup and the ground, Mercy I asked, mercy I found' (William Camden, 'Epitaph for a Man Killed by Falling from his Horse').

grand enough i.e. good enough, superior enough.

dumb i.e. stupid.

paddock Frog or toad.

You took me up wrong You misunderstood me.

with the joy of a besieged man This again is cinematic, the climax to so many films of the time.

It was worth murdering a world In Pinkie's diseased mind, he thinks that killing and more killing would be worthwhile in order to escape being tied sexually to a woman.

gave to a dirty act This indeed shows his bias against sexual love.

pull-ins i.e. where cars or coaches stopped by the roadside.

A Night of Love The slot machines with suggestive pictures – perhaps thought wicked in the 1930s, but dull by the standards of today's permissiveness.

there was Spicer The importance of the photograph makes the Boy determined to kill Spicer.

hypo Hyposulphite of soda, used in photography for fixing a negative.

by-your-leave Permission.

King Edward VIII (Prince of Wales) This is probably – in the context of the other associations in the sentence – a misprint for Edward VII (ruled 1901–10).

Vesta Tilley A music-hall star.

Henry Irving The legendary Shakespearean actor and producer.

Lily Langtry Actress and famous beauty.

Mrs Pankhurst One of the leaders of the suffragette movement early in the century.

Spicer was among the immortals At this stage only in terms of a photograph; but the phrase holds ominous suggestions of what is to come.

a leather-jacket ... she loves me not Greene is rather inaccurate here: a leather-jacket is the *grub* of the crane-fly – he obviously meant an adult crane-fly. This is, however, a fine sequence, which mirrors the whole action of the novel – the crane-fly being Hale; the watch-spring recording time; the dismembering, the Boy's capacity for violence; and the last words an ironic reversal of what Rose really feels for him.

There ... racket Pinkie means that Spicer thoughtlessly walked into trouble.

stuck on you i.e. loves you.

tracks Race-tracks.

not set for the flames i.e. not going to hell.

nickers in the till Pounds saved up.

calcined i.e. desiccated, dried cut.

thés dansants i.e. a tea-dance, with small orchestra.

board-school i.e. state elementary school.

Part 4

Chapter 1

It is the Saturday of the races in Brighton. Pinkie goes down to the course with Spicer, pondering whether or not to ensure Rose's silence by marrying her. Spicer bets on an ominously named horse (Memento Mori), but the race is won by Black Boy. Just after that Calleoni's mob attacks, and for good measure they 'carve up' Pinkie as well. Though pursued, Pinkie escapes, and hides in a garage, the associations of which he hates. He makes his way back to Snow's, and meets Rose in a cellar, where she brings him water to wash with. Pinkie believes that Spicer is dead, and in the restaurant he hears Ida's laugh. Meanwhile the manageress comes down and interrupts them, and Pinkie returns to his bed-sitting room, where he tells Cubitt what has happened to Spicer; he also orders him to send for Prewitt, the lawyer. When the latter arrives Pinkie questions him about the ways of getting married, despite the fact that he is under age. Then Dallow returns with the news that Spicer is in his room, and not dead as Pinkie had thought.

harboured it i.e. kept it.

in Indian file In single file, as in the manner of American Indians.

like those of pit ponies Again the unifying references – here a reminiscence of old Crowe.

amok Madly, chaotically.

armadillos South American burrowing animals, with body encased in armour.

a Packard Vintage car of superior manufacture.

like an Underground staircase An escalator (a 'moving staircase') in London's Underground railway.

totsies Slang, dated word for 'girls'.

ordure Mess, excreta.

dividers i.e. measuring compasses, used in geometry – or for stabbing

the man who believed in a second coming A religious 'crank' either with a placard or haranguing people as they pass.

a tied house i.e. one maintained by one brewery only and selling its beer only.

plantains Low herb with broad flat leaves spread out close to the ground; often found as a weed in lawns.

Tattersall Associated with horse-dealing, and a betting rendezvous.

take a plunge Have a bet.

as easy as shelling peas Simple.

Memento Mori (L.) 'Remember you must die.' A reminder of death.

A pony £25.

perked me up i.e. made me happier.

game i.e. carried on until.

masonic passes A reference to the fact that freemasons make certain signs to each other to indicate that they belong to the 'brotherhood'.

bookies Bookmakers.

the censer swung ... intoned the winners Note the mixture, in Pinkie's mind, of religious ritual and the commonplace of racing – indicating his confusion and uncertainty.

cruelty straightening his body like lust The second time that a sexual image has been used to describe the reactions of the determinedly anti-sexual Pinkie.

tout i.e. someone selling tips for the races.

jackdaw i.e. one who steals, here collects, things.

cruel virginity Another variation to describe Pinkie's state.

One confession ... In his time of defeat, Pinkie recurs to his religion, promising himself that he will wipe out all his sins.

Regency Square In the period of the Prince Regent – late 18th/early 19th century – before he became George IV (1820–30).

a Lancia A superior Italian car, symbol of Pinkie's humiliation, here because Mr Colleoni, or his equivalent, is inside it; later because it is in a Lancia that Pinkie fails to make love to a girl.

the alignments at Waterloo The great battle in 1815 in which Wellington and Blücher (the Prussian general) defeated Napoleon.

circumspect Cautious, cunning.

henna A red hair-dye made from the shoots and leaves of a tropical shrub.

skirt A cheap way of referring to a girl.

smutty Dirty, suggestive.

soft as butter i.e. oily, persuasive.

damp Catherine wheel A type of spinning firework.

burnt i.e. went to Hell.

on the Austrian hock Note that Greene constantly reverts to
the wine in the cellar in this sequence – and that wine is an
essential part of Roman Catholic ritual – a ritual constantly
present in Pinkie's mind.

followers i.e. young men courting (you).

carious Decayed (teeth). Again the word is symbolic of their
way of life.

You dog, you i.e. you're a bit of a devil.

wangle Deception.

many victories ... defeats An index to Prewitt's character –
the fact that he is dishonest, crooked.

you've been in the wars i.e. you've been in trouble.

Hard and fast i.e. completely, indissolubly.

a minor's In the 1930s a minor would be someone under the
age of 21.

Moss's Moss Brothers, the firm which hires out clothes for
particular occasions, like weddings etc.

spouse His way of saying 'wife'. When we see her later, we
understand the self-irony of this affectation.

at the game In this instance, he means 'marriage'.

spliced Married.

Chapter 2

Ida in Snow's, determined to find out all she can from Rose.
They discuss 'right and wrong', but Ida can't get Rose to
divulge anything of interest.

like a warship ... every man would do his duty A curious
mixture; for large women, the association with battleships is a
commonplace, but here we have added the cliché about the
1914–18 War ('the war to end all wars') and Nelson's
instructions to his men at Trafalgar.

in train i.e. organized.

at a public i.e. a public house.

the child Again a recurrence to the *youth* of Rose (an equivalent

to Pinkie's being consistently called the Boy); also indicative of
Rose's vulnerability.

Puritan i.e. narrow-minded.

the girdle of Venus Symbolic here of her sensuality.

driven to her hole the small animal peered Part of the
imagery of the novel, underlining the sordid nature of these
deprived lives.

Chapter 3

Spicer has had an 'accident'; Pinkie contemplates his body
at the foot of the stairs. Pinkie tells Prewitt he is to say that
he saw what happened, and that only he and Dallow (but
not Pinkie) were there. Pinkie goes to Snow's, and finds Rose
in the room talking to Ida, who warns Rose, saying that she
hasn't 'finished with' them. Pinkie tells Rose that he is going
to marry her.

spreadeagled like Prometheus One of the Titans,
Prometheus stole fire from the Gods. He was punished by being
chained to a rock, where an eagle chewed his liver, which grew
again each night. Note that a 'walnut-stained' eagle is across the
body here.

like trains on the inner circle The Circle line on the London
Underground railway.

like the little man in the bowler The image evokes the
legendary comedian Charlie Chaplin, and the triumph of the
underdog over the brutality of bullies.

badly foxed Having brown stains.

Van Tromp's victory A reference to the famous Dutch admiral
who defeated the English fleet in the Straits of Dover in 1652,
and sailed down the Channel with a broom at his masthead.

the pictures or maybe ... the front The limits of Rose's
romantic desires exposed – at the cinema, or on the sea-front.

like a blind girl, for further alms A pathetic image of Rose.

like a room or a chair Again, Pinkie's capacity to
depersonalize others is stressed.

Part 5

Chapter 1

The inquest on Spicer is over, and Pinkie thinks back to the death of their lost leader Kite. Dallow and Pinkie go out to the Queen of Hearts to celebrate; the first person they see is Spicer's girl. After some talk she and Pinkie go to the car park and choose a Lancia, but Pinkie cannot make love to her.

The blind band They have appeared previously, and symbolize the extent of Pinkie's inhumanity, though he is 'shocked by his own action' in pushing the leader out of the way.

a pick-up i.e. something to restore your spirits.

bottled up i.e. brooding.

like a cuttlefish This emits a dark liquid.

like candles ... the iron nave ... half vulture and half dove Again the description suggests the divisions within Pinkie – the call of religion on the one hand and the urge to destroy and tear on the other.

a blow Trip in the fresh air.

a windmill i.e. one converted into a teashop.

dicky Back of car arranged as extra seat or for luggage.

class i.e. superior.

clapping Talking.

took her reluctantly in Gazed at her, sized her up.

Sidecar A favourite cocktail of the thirties.

first shot At once, first time.

jerk you up i.e. cheer you up.

lamp i.e. look at.

the smashed village and the ravaged woman i.e. the terrible experiences, the reality that follows any plan.

shaker Cocktail shaker, for mixing the drinks.

gin slings Another alcoholic drink much favoured in the thirties.

and the game Prostitution.

Mr Colleoni bowed like a shopwalker Pinkie's ambitions are
translated imaginatively into the humiliations of Colleoni.

You've got the doings? This question really exposes Pinkie's
ignorance and inexperience; Sylvie assumes that he is taking
contraceptive precautions.

swam together stroke by stroke Symbolic of their harmony
and implying the sexual union of which Pinkie has just
demonstrated himself incapable.

Chapter 2

On the way back Pinkie resists the idea of marriage, but
when he arrives he finds that Rose is waiting for him; she
has found the photographer's snap of Spicer in the local
paper, and realizes the fact that Pinkie has lied to her about
Spicer being killed on the course. Rose has been sacked for
being rude to a customer – Ida; Pinkie returns to the idea of
marriage.

as if the handcuffs were meeting An image that is to recur,
and which is to characterize Pinkie's fear.

like the guns in a Q ship The name given, in the First World
War, to innocent-looking tramp steamers with concealed guns.

her carved devotion Ironic again, in view of the emphasis on
'carving' in its other sense.

Chapter 3

Pinkie goes to Nelson Place, where Rose lives, and meets
her parents in their sordid, deprived surroundings. He
arranges to pay them fifteen guineas if they will give their
consent to Rose's marrying him.

verdigrised Rusted over with green.

the shabby secret behind the bright corsage i.e. the streets which lie behind the impressive façade of Brighton are sordid and dirty.

shingle i.e. hair done in a particular fashion.

I'll settle them I'll deal with them.

gave out like a gramophone i.e. stopped speaking, just as a gramophone winds down.

the game to the last card i.e. kept up the act to the end.

Chapter 4

Ida with Phil Corkery in the Pompadour Boudoir; Mr Colleoni passes by, and Ida suggests to Phil that they stay there for 'a bit of fun'. Ida books a room on the strength of her winnings on Black Boy.

boskages Woody retreats.

Distinguay Distinguished: an uncultured anglicization of the French word *distingué(e)*.

desired or dreaded her assent Mr Corkery shares with Pinkie some uncertainty about his sexual performance.

Half and half i.e. we'll share expenses.

aphrodisiac i.e. promoting sexual desire.

Bacchic Drinking, sensual mood (from Bacchus, the god of wine).

carnival i.e. for enjoying herself.

pleasure dome A reminiscence of 'Kubla Khan' by Samuel Taylor Coleridge (1772–1834): 'In Xanadu did Kubla Khan/A stately pleasure dome decree.'

a dead crab beaten and broken Symbolic of the predatory aspect of life, in nature and in man.

Chapter 5

Cubitt is a little drunk, celebrating Pinkie's forthcoming marriage. Pinkie has a drink, then receives presents from Cubitt; he is angry at their nature, and nearly gives away the fact that he has killed Spicer. Cubitt is suspicious, though, and decides to clear out.

lean hungry faces A reminiscence of Cassius in *Julius Caesar*.
And, of course, this is a group of conspirators.

Titian Golden, auburn, named after the painter of that name.

moued Pouted.

in a kip Probably a reference to the fact that Rose 'slept in' at
Snow's.

laying i.e. having sex with her.

commode A low, wooden (usually mahogany) chair,
incorporating a lavatory for invalids.

A.1 First-class.

rough houses i.e. fights.

like I treated Spicer This gives away the fact that Pinkie is
implicated in Spicer's death, something that Cubitt would not
have known for certain.

Taj Mahal A magnificent mausoleum erected in Agra, north-
west India by the Emperor Shah Jehan for himself and his
favourite wife.

haemophilia Hereditary tendency to bleed heavily from the
slightest injury.

Chapter 6

Ida after love-making; she is dissatisfied with Phil Corkery's
performance, but continues to plan her campaign, deciding
that she must get hold of one of Pinkie's gang.

Men always failed you ... to the pictures The implication is
that Ida is full-blooded and highly sexed, but has to make do
with second-hand life as portrayed in the cinema.

Bohemian Socially unconventional, of free and easy habits.

Part 6

Chapter 1

Cubitt is getting drunk and talking mysteriously. He thinks about the idea of going to see Colleoni to tell him that he has finished with Pinkie. Eventually he goes in quest of Colleoni at The Cosmopolitan, but is headed off by Crab, who tells him Calleoni could not use him – though he, Crab, will put in a good word for him. But when Crab leaves, Cubitt is picked up by Ida, who buys him a drink and begins to elicit from him the information she needs, i.e. that Spicer left the card and that his 'accident' has been faked by Pinkie. She also learns that Pinkie is to marry Rose. She confirms in her own mind that Fred was murdered.

like Narcissus into his pool The youth in classical mythology who fell in love with his own image in a pool and pined away.

sibilitation Hissing sound(s).

Two leaden football teams They can be moved when a coin is inserted in the machine.

A Love Letter Another slot machine. When a coin is inserted, it will provide a love letter.

Pet ... Spooner Terms for kissing, cuddling.

Cupid The Roman God of Love, represented as a beautiful boy.

Amor *Amour*, French for 'love'.

gave you the air i.e. discarded you.

Loved and Lost An ironic echo of Tennyson's ' 'Tis better to have loved and lost/Than never to have loved at all' (from *In Memoriam*).

pomade Scented ointment for skin and hair.

Doncaster There is a famous racecourse here.

Tuileries A former royal palace, still to be seen in Paris; Louis XVI lived there after his arrest during the French Revolution.

marquetry Inlaid work.

clean up this track i.e. make this racecourse protection racket respectable (obviously by eliminating Pinkie's mob).

Havana A reference to the quality of the cigar.

I think of your wondrous, winsome This is in Cubitt's consciousness – a quotation from the love letter he got from the machine.

a courtyard ... a cock crowing Peter's denial of Jesus is obviously implied here.

cleaned out i.e. broke, having no money.

Chapter 2

This section marks the marriage of Pinkie and Rose. Afterwards they go to a pub round the corner; then Pinkie insists they go to The Cosmopolitan. There they are snubbed – there are obviously no double rooms available for their kind and age – and they set off, Pinkie bitterly humiliated, for Billy's. But first Pinkie makes a recorded message for Rose (damning her in words when she thinks it is a message of love). He buys her some Brighton rock and they go to the pictures. After that they eventually arrive at Billy's, go to Pinkie's room, and make love. But Pinkie is disturbed by the return of Cubitt, who tries to get back into favour with him. Pinkie returns to Rose and dreams of his childhood. When he gets up he goes for a walk, and finds a loving note from Rose in his pocket.

the mare and the stallion Notice the reduction to crude animalism and the association with horse-racing.

Film Fun A comic of the period, using as cartoon characters the stars of films and radio.

the rules i.e. of sex.

Bouncing and ploughing A description of his mother and father in the sexual act.

malaria Tropical disease caused by mosquito bites; it can recur throughout life.

on the line i.e. the railway line.

Lady Angeline ... expose herself thus Pinkie is speaking of

romantic sentimental novelettes on the one hand and perversion
on the other: both are, to him, aspects of the detested word
'love'.

Credo in unum Satanum I believe in one Satan: a perversion
of the opening words of the Nicene Creed used in the Anglican
and Roman Catholic Churches.

gaudy statues in an ugly church Note again the religious
reference, particularly a Roman Catholic one.

in a state of grace i.e. free from sin.

he had put away childish things See 1 Corinthians, 13,11:
'When I became a man, I put away childish things.'

Roses, roses all the way, and never a sprig of yew A
combination of Browning's 'The Patriot' and Matthew Arnold's
'Requiescat' ('And never a sprig of yew').

covenants Agreements.

his temporal safety ... two immortalities of pain His
safety on earth for the two murders he had committed.

the market was firm i.e. there were more weddings coming.

We're up in the sanctuary Pinkie can't get the religious
ceremony that might have been out of his mind.

an Eden of ignorance Fine ironic phrase: a contrast with the
real Eden, which was synonymous with innocence before the
Fall.

as if a crime had been committed And in a sense it has in
this particular 'marriage'.

Pullman i.e. first-class rail travel.

Stickphast Glue.

this kip stinks This place is beneath our contempt.

Had he got to massacre a world? Pinkie is psychopathic, in
miniature like a diseased dictator; Greene almost anticipates
here the powerful psychopath who did massacre a world, i.e.
Hitler.

soft i.e. silly, sentimental.

graven on vulcanite i.e. reproduced on a record.

a stick of Brighton rock This of course reminds Pinkie of the
killing of Fred Hale.

like you got God in the Eucharist i.e. the presence of God in
the Holy Communion.

coracles Small waterproofed wickerwork boats of a distinctive rounded shape, still used in Wales and Ireland.

like cats A reference to the stalking of one another by the lovers on the screen.

a blonde with Garbo cheeks A reference to the beauty of the legendary Swedish film star Greta Garbo, a great favourite in the 1930s.

A bell tolled An ominous death association – and to be alone with Rose is a kind of death to Pinkie.

your cave It is in Pinkie's consciousness – almost a reversion to the state of primitive man.

a cry of pain An indication that Rose is a virgin.

He had graduated He had proved himself sexually.

unshriven Unabsolved from sin, his confession unheard.

his glasses i.e. the number of drinks he had consumed.

as if he had outsoared the shadow of any night An echo, perhaps deliberate, of Shelley's *Adonais: an elergy on the death of John Keats* – 'He has outsoared the shadow of our night' (the opening lines of Stanza 40).

that's rich i.e. that's a good joke.

not a pin i.e. nothing.

the piece of gold in the palm Another mingling of the religious associations of marriage with the sordid reality.

He was in an asphalt playground ... a razor in his hand The paragraph of this dream sequence is a fine psychological integration of Pinkie, a tracing of the journey from fear to moral degradation and violence.

as irrevocable as a sacrament Again the religious reference.

it might prove useful one day Pinkie does retain the slip of paper, and thinks of using it in the 'suicide' of Rose.

Blessed art thou among women The old woman is saying her Rosary – and is therefore among the saved; Pinkie is beyond prayer, and is therefore damned.

Part 7

Chapter 1

Rose wakes alone and explores the room, the landing, the stairs. She meets Judy and Dallow, and feels accepted in the house. Later she goes to Snow's, and tells one of the girls that she is married; on the way back she sees Dallow, who tells her that her mother has come to visit her. It is, as we might guess, Ida who has come in search of more information: she wants a word with Pinkie. She tells Rose that Pinkie is a murderer, but Rose remains adamant and reveals nothing; Ida further tells her that she may have a murderer's baby unless she takes precautions.

if she barks If she complains.
Liberty Hall i.e. where you are free to do anything.
prehensile Capable of grasping, seizing.
gets worked up i.e. angry.
no sooner ... past the customs ... naturalization papers were signed Always the wider range of reference, here to refugees leaving their own land as a result of persecution – a common manifestation in the 1930s, with Hitler's attacks on the Jews.
There's a duck i.e. there's a good girl.
hubby Husband.
Matins Morning prayers.
outside, looking in The phrase symbolizes their state – hers and Pinkie's – for just as they are outside society so they are outside their religion, in sin.
not all roses i.e. not all easy and pleasant.
on the vulcanite On the gramophone record (which Pinkie has made).
rattled i.e. worried.
to let you be i.e. to leave you as you are.
Like an idiot's ... a bombed home Again the contemporary

associations are apparent. The Spanish Civil War, or Mussolini's attack on Abyssinia would provide instances; and with typical Greene economy he has 'photographed' such a scene in words.

hung up among the wreaths discordantly Ida has been sad and mournful so far on Rose's account; but now that she is angry there is discord.

cleared for action … the map of a campaign By these oblique images Greene is conveying the fact that war is near.

aphorism Short, sharp remark.

getting warm i.e. close to discovering all.

Chapter 2

Pinkie watches Ida leave, then catches Rose out in a lie – she says it was her Mum who has called. Pinkie goes down to the basement with Dallow, drops the flower he was holding, and thinks about Rose, weighing up the advantages of killing her. He wants to make it appear that Rose has killed herself. When he returns upstairs Rose admits that it was Ida who has visited her; Pinkie thinks that she has seen the flower, and that this has provoked her confession, but he promises that he will take care of everything.

Have I got to have that massacre? Again the reiterated expression of a need; Pinkie does not outwardly answer himself, but knows inwardly that he must go on killing.

carve … boiling i.e. use my razor on the whole lot.

little piece Girl.

stake you a fiver she's straight Bet you five pounds that she won't betray you.

a bad replica A poor imitation.

his dark suggestion i.e. of death.

Chapter 3

Pinkie goes out, to discover whether his lawyer Prewitt has seen Ida; Prewitt is largely broken by events, knows that

Colleoni is going to take over, and confides his unhappiness – marital and otherwise – to Pinkie. He talks self-importantly, and this worries Pinkie, for he sees what Prewitt could reveal if pressed. He persuades him to take a holiday in France, promising him £20, with more to follow; Prewitt agrees to leave next day.

Rex i.e. the crown, the prosecution.

Eat, drink, for tomorrow Prewitt tactfully does not finish the quotation. Had he done so he would have added 'we die'.

How now! a rat? The first of the many associations (in Part 7) with *Hamlet*. This is from Act III, Scene 4, where Hamlet kills Polonius.

The rank, intruding fool From the same scene in *Hamlet*, though 'rank' should read 'rash'.

What ho, ole mole! Again not a direct quotation, but referring to *Hamlet*, Act I, Scene 5.

A swell i.e. of superior birth and position, status.

thrown my sponge in yet i.e. surrendered, given up.

to unburden myself i.e. get things off my chest, confide in you.

bonhomie (From the French); geniality, good nature.

Why, this is Hell From Marlowe's *Dr Faustus* (c.1588).

like Samson i.e. having immense strength.

esprit de corps Regard for honour.

that mole in the cellarage Another reference to *Hamlet*.

No money can heal a mind diseased 'Minister to a mind diseased' is from *Macbeth*, Act V, Scene 3, and refers to Lady Macbeth's illness.

I have done the state some service *Othello*, Act V, Scene 2.

Chapter 4

Pinkie tells Dallow to watch Prewitt's, goes back to his room and finds that Rose has cleared up; when she hears a baby crying she feels that she may have a child, their child – much to Pinkie's disgust.

to thrust the lesson Note the immediate sexual association – and remember that Pinkie has 'graduated'.

vicarious agony Suffering on another's account.

Chapter 5

Next morning Pinkie sees Dallow. Rose goes out, and Dallow comes back to say that he thinks they will soon hear that Prewitt is on the boat. Colleoni has offered to buy Pinkie out. Then the phone message comes through to say that Prewitt has gone.

suckers Mugs, people who can be easily duped.

Goodwood ... Hurst Park ... Newmarket All prominent racecourses.

coition Sexual intercourse.

Chapter 6

Ida in the tea-room with Phil. She is watching Pinkie and Rose, Dallow and Judy; she also talks to Phil and reminisces about the people she has saved in the past.

all passion spent Milton's *Samson Agonistes*, line 1745.

Chapter 7

Pinkie is watching Ida; then he and Rose go for a stroll, and he reminds her that the tea-room is where they first met. He suggests a drive into the country, then he plants the idea in an attendant's mind that they are going by bus to Peacehaven. Actually they go by car, and Pinkie talks to Rose of a suicide pact between them which he will arrange. Rose feels that he is 'a thousand miles away'. They go to a hotel and are served by Piker, whom Pinkie used to bully at school. He persuades Rose to add that she 'couldn't live without' him, to the note he already has in her handwriting. He prepares the revolver.

get your rag out Lose your temper.
an outer i.e. the outside ring on the target.
a freshener i.e. something to cheer (us) up.
planted The word suggests, inevitably, the earlier 'planting' of the card by Spicer.
the rent Tear or hole.
the cuffs i.e. handcuffs.
Dona nobis pacem Give us peace.
pipe-dream Fantastic.
Lureland i.e. an entertainment hall or amusement arcade.
breaks i.e. when they went out to 'play'.
the huge darkness pressed a wet mouth against the panes A fine personification, at once sensual and symbolic of the darkness in which the characters, and particularly Pinkie, are enshrouded.

Chapter 8

Meanwhile, back at the tea-rooms Dallow and Judy are still waiting for Pinkie and Rose; Ida approaches them, and reminds Dallow that he had followed her – and Fred – in his old Morris on the fateful day. She also tells him that Prewitt is at the police station. Judy comes to interrupt the conversation, but despite the offer of £20, Dallow won't say anything. Dallow learns that Pinkie has gone, goes in search of his Morris, and realizes that Pinkie has taken it. When he sees Ida again, it is apparent that Pinkie has taken Rose away with the intention of killing her; Ida insists that they hire a car and go in pursuit.

barnacled Covered, adhered to.
a drain i.e. going to the lavatory.
gammy i.e. lame, crippled.
lit up Drunk.

Chapter 9

Pinkie is in the hotel, listening to the conversation of two rather superior people, who go out; then Pinkie and Rose leave too. He asks her if she wants to kill herself first, and then goes away to leave her to it. Rose is about to raise the gun against herself when she hears a voice shout 'Pinkie'; feeling this may mean good news, she throws the gun away. Pinkie attempts to use the vitriol, but a policeman's baton breaks the bottle, and Pinkie receives the acid in his own face. He runs, and falls into the sea.

gambits i.e. affected actions.
we touched eighty i.e. reached eighty miles (129 km) per hour.
a good bus A good car.
sting you i.e. charge you.
She's hot i.e. she'll give us a good time.
the Laughing Cavalier A reminiscence of Prewitt's jocular greeting of Pinkie earlier. The portrait is by Franz Hals, the eminent Dutch painter (1580–1666).
you plan to fight in Spain Another reference to important contemporary events – here the Spanish Civil War which ended in a victory for General Franco.
Herod seeking the child's birthplace i.e. after the foretelling of the birth of Christ.
badgered i.e. nagged at.

Chapter 10

Ida sorts out the loose ends of the story over a drink. She had made up the part about Prewitt being at the police station, and she has probably lost Phil Corkery because of her obstinacy in pursuing Pinkie. She returns to Russell Square where she and old Crowe consult the Board again.

hold on i.e. keep going.

Sui Ida now associates what the Board 'said' with Pinkie's action.

points shift i.e. in the signal-box.

there's more things in heaven and earth Another reference to *Hamlet*, Act I, Scene 5.

Chapter 11

Rose at confession, not forgetting Pinkie but regretting that she didn't kill herself. The priest tells her of the 'strangeness of the mercy of God', and urges her that if there is a baby, 'make him a saint – to pray for his father'. Rose goes back to Billy's, to what Greene calls 'the worst horror of all' – for she treasures the idea of hearing Pinkie's recorded message to her.

eucalyptus Oil from the tree, disinfectant.

Corruptio optimi est pessima The more excellent the man, the sadder his downfall.

the horror of the complete circle i.e. that she is back where she had started.

Revision questions

1 How does Graham Greene succeed in creating atmosphere in *Brighton Rock*?

2 Write a considered character analysis of Pinkie. In what ways does he appear to you to be abnormal?

3 Write an essay on Greene's use of figurative language in *Brighton Rock*.

4 Compare and contrast the characters of Dallow and Cubitt.

5 Compare and contrast the characters of Fred Hale and Prewitt.

6 Write an appreciation of Greene's use of slang or song or quotation in the novel.

7 In what ways do you find *Brighton Rock* a profoundly depressing book?

8 Do you find Ida a completely sympathetic character, or not? Give reasons for your answer by referring closely to the text.

9 In what ways is *Brighton Rock* an exciting novel?

10 Write an account of the part played by Rose in the development of the plot.

11 What is the author telling us about human nature in this novel?

12 By a close look at the novel, say why you think Greene's work is excellent material for a play or film.

13 Do you regard *Brighton Rock* as 'merely cynical'?

14 What qualities in Greene's style make him a poetic writer?

15 'Dull': how would you defend *Brighton Rock* from this charge?

16 By referring closely to the novel, give examples of Greene's eye and ear for detail in his descriptions.

17 'It lacks humour.' Would you agree with this statement about *Brighton Rock*?

18 'Dated, and not really an "entertainment".' Do you agree with this opinion of the novel?

19 In what ways do you find *Brighton Rock* disturbing?

20 Compare this novel with any other you have read, either by Greene or which has been written in the last thirty years.

Pan study aids

Titles published in the Brodie's Notes series

W. H. Auden Selected Poetry

Jane Austen Emma Mansfield Park Northanger Abbey Persuasion
Pride and Prejudice

Anthologies of Poetry The Metaphysical Poets The Poet's Tale

Samuel Beckett Waiting for Godot

Arnold Bennett The Old Wives' Tale

William Blake Songs of Innocence and Experience

Robert Bolt A Man for All Seasons

Harold Brighouse Hobson's Choice

Charlotte Brontë Jane Eyre

Emily Brontë Wuthering Heights

John Bunyan The Pilgrim's Progress

Geoffrey Chaucer The Pardoner's Tale
(**parallel text editions**) The Franklin's Tale The Knight's Tale
The Miller's Tale The Nun's Priest's Tale The Pardoner's Tale
Prologue to the Canterbury Tales The Wife of Bath's Tale

John Clare Selected Poetry and Prose

William Congreve The Way of the World

Joseph Conrad The Nigger of the Narcissus & Youth
Heart of Darkness

Charles Dickens Dombey and Son Great Expectations
Hard Times Little Dorrit Oliver Twist Our Mutual Friend
A Tale of Two Cities

George Eliot Middlemarch The Mill on the Floss Silas Marner

T. S. Eliot Murder in the Cathedral Selected Poems

Henry Fielding Joseph Andrews

F. Scott Fitzgerald The Great Gatsby

E. M. Forster Howard's End A Passage to India

William Golding Lord of the Flies The Spire

Student's notes